TED'S STORY

ALAN ROBSON MBE

Britain's Next
BESTSELLER

First published in 2018 by:

Britain's Next Bestseller
An imprint of Live It Ventures LTD
27 Old Gloucester Road
London.
WC1N 3AX

All enquiries should be addressed to info@bnbsbooks.co.uk

Cover design by vikncharlie

www.bnbsbooks.co.uk
@BNBSbooks

Dedicated to everyone I've met on an incredible journey with people from all over the world including my beloved North!

THE GREATEST STORY NEVER TOLD…

Working as a Talk Show host on the radio brings you into the lives of millions of people and very occasionally, someone who changes your whole world.

It was a day like any other when Heather, our receptionist at Metro Radio/TFM, tells me there is a young, rather agitated, man, desperate to talk to me. Despite being in the middle of a busy afternoon of interviews, sessions and prep, I popped down. The young lad said his name was Anthony and he had a story he wanted to tell the world.

Somewhat dubious, I asked what story he referred to. He said his Grandfather was a hero in the war.

My father served proudly in World War Two and I had thought I should, one day, tell his tale of North Africa, then the assault into Italy, including the battle at Monte Casino. Truthfully, so many did far more than him, valiant though he was.

Anthony stuttered out the words then opened an envelope saying, "But he wrote it all down!"

I half expected a manuscript that I could read and decide if I could do anything with it. Instead, inside a filthy clip file, were very old folded scraps of paper and about fifteen sketches similar to those a ten-year-old could do.

The sketches were enough for me to thank him but send him on his way. But something, to this day I still don't know what, made me stop.

There on a scrunched and folded bit of paper, written in super sharp pencil, were not stories, but rather bullet points.

- Natives saw children, young girls to rape later.
- We watched as they risked their lives and that of their families, to murder Japanese Officers and sneak away.
- We saw them sneak them out one by one.
- The bravest thing I ever saw, feel ashamed we never did it!

After reading the first one, I unfolded the second piece of paper and the third and the fourth. After about ten, the file was empty.

I told the young man that what he had was terrific, but add them all together and I could read them in about ten minutes. They were random, no definitive time scale, so there was no way to tie them together in any way accurately.

He looked completely flattened, having already tried to find a publisher, or a TV or film company.

"Me Mams got lots more!" he proclaimed "And she's got lung cancer and to wants to tell everyone his story. It's the one thing she wants to do before she dies."

Feeling the boys pain, I thought I would give him a bit of encouragement.

"Look, I can't promise anything, but you get me everything from your Mum and any other information from other relatives about this man. Once I see how much you have, I'll be able to tell you if I can do anything with it!"

Cheered by this, he walked off and I never saw him again.

So, in my bottomless cupboards, the kind anorak keeps everything 'just in case'.

It lay there for almost a year.

Then our trusty receptionist handed me a filthy Co-Operative society carrier bag. In it were a couple of letters about a ladies Dad (who died in WW2) and two others from ex-forces personnel telling stories as to how these two best friends saved their lives.

Beneath the newly written letters were about five hundred folded scraps of paper, many never opened since they were scrunched and hidden from the Japanese in one of their death camps known as Tamajao's.

With them, was a beautifully tender note from the man's daughter, now battling cancer, talking about how kind and lovely her Daddy had been. She even told how her Dad visited his best friend's wife after the war to return his few belongings.

Realising what they were and who they belonged to, I decided I needed to do something with them. The problem was that I had no way of contacting Anthony. Instead, I went and put appeals out on air without success.

I had been given real treasure, an unknown story of two men clinging to life at the hands of the Japanese.

I ended up spending almost three months learning the history timeline so I could attach these tiny tales to the period they happened.

Some of the stories merely painted details of particular Japanese soldiers and how you could tell which ones were likely to kill you.

Others were incredible stories of daring do.

As the war stretched out, the stories became longer and more fluent. After almost eight months I roughly had everything where it historically fit.

The problem now was thatI could not confirm whether the names of the Allied and Japanese soldiers were real.

I needed more.

Three days before Christmas there was a phone call to my producer at the time, asking for the stories back. I returned them to the carrier bag and left them at reception; I asked that whoever collected them call me urgently.

No one ever did.

So here I was, very frustrated while I scanned my notes and saw the number of the Tamajao. My memory was flickering; I was remembering seeing the word before.

But where?

I went back through those files I keep about everything and there was a little booklet published by a soldier named Ernest Warwick. I had interviewed him on the radio show and as a thank you, he sent me his self-published book.

I started reading it and to my surprise, ALL the Japanese soldiers named by Anthony's Grandfather were there! Every one confirmed by Ernie Warwick. No mention of the Allied troops in the next door camp, but it seems the Japanese Officers ran several camps at once.

All I needed now was to link the pieces. Yes, much would remain missing, but surely that would be the nature of these camps. Most days nothing significant would happen and then, occasionally, something horrific would occur.

I booked tickets to fly to Thailand and visited the actual site of the camp in order to to tell Anthony's Grandfather's story with respect.

Everyday up until then, often into the early hours of

dawn, I would try to make the story seamless. It ultimately, in my opinion, became one of the most horrific, yet courageous stories ever told.

Maybe it's the LAST GREAT UNTOLD STORY OF WORLD WAR TWO

It has been my honour to put it together to share with you.

Chapter 1

MALAYSIA

There he was, looking better than he had for years.

His hair was blowing off his face and his cheeks were reddened for the first time in so very long.

He was looking straight at Ted Morris, his best friend.

They had joined up together, sailed out to Singapore side by side and had vowed to get back home together too. Alec Smith was a Scot from Edinburgh and more than anything he wanted to get back there as soon as he could. His young wife, Maggie and his two children Jean and Alexander, were counting the days until he was returned to them.

They loved him so much, especially little Jean who was a daddy's girl.

Ted stared into his friend's eyes as Alec smiled at him. It was one of those smiles that makes you feel that everything is going to be alright. There was a silence as if all of time and space had stopped; there was only a single connection between two best friends.

Ted found himself smiling too.

Alec was a good man, a great friend and a wonderful father. The world was better for him being in it.

Ted found himself mouthing goodbye to his friend. It had not sunk in that Alec's head was eight feet from his body.

Then, as swift as the sword that decapitated him, his eyes just glazed over as all life finally escaped him. The ground beneath Ted was now soggy with the blood oozing from the lifeless body of the most significant friend he had ever known.

How long before Ted would join him?

This is merely five minutes of Ted's story.

Chapter 2

T he world was a tumbling catalogue of misery back in January 1942.

The German's were pushing back the 8th Army in North Africa, millions of Jews were being raped, brutalised and exterminated in the death camps, America was still in a state of shock over the Pearl Harbour bombings and tiny Britain seemed to be all that stood against the evil in the world.

Back in England, all unmarried men between the ages of 20 and 70 were being called up. Ted had travelled to Singapore with his battalion to reinforce an Australian detachment who admitted they could not imagine holding out against a far superior Japanese force.

The place was known across the world as the Fortress of Singapore, but did not feel like it. Pearl Harbour had forced the Japanese to launch massive attacks right across South East Asia. Hong Kong in China had fallen after a bloody, seven-day onslaught. There, 6000 brave soldiers surrendered and almost 170 of their Officers were decapitated as a warning to their men not to defy their conquerors.

Within days they had taken the Islands of Guam and Wake, as battles continued to take Luzon, the largest island of the Philippines. The American forces that had hurriedly raced there could not stop the massive Japanese army.

With that miserable and terrifying backdrop, it was hard to understand how these British soldiers marching into the city were laughing and joking.

Ted shouted, "Come on Aussie stop hiding, we'll protect you."

The cowering Australian soldier smiled and shouted back "You Poms better get your heads down before these buggers take them off!"

The Commanding Officer was a stiff-backed jobsworth called Aitken and he would not let them take shelter. He stood them all at attention in an open square and asked an Australian to fetch his Commanding Officer.

"He's dead sir" came the reply.

On asking who was now in charge, the young Australian merely shrugged his shoulders. Just then there was a gunshot some distance away and a bullet sliced through the chest of Aitken. Strangely, you were able to hear the bullet zip through the webbing and cloth of his uniform and into the body of the Englishman.

He staggered a little as blood began to trickle through.

"Take cover men and be smart about it"

The Australians were used to the countless snipers as the Japanese had the entire area in a magnificent crossfire. They were happy to let whole battalions in, but no one could get out.

Aitken refused to dive for cover; merely marching toward a building as at least a half a dozen bullets whizzed past his head.

Ted wrote:

"Some of these Officers may well have been toffs, but you could not fault their courage. Aitken had ice in his veins. I saw bullets taking branches off trees as he walked past and at one point, almost gave the Jap's a sitting duck to shoot at as he stood still facing the tree line some hundred yards away. As he did, there were even more shots and he walked on. He had some brass!"

Ted and Alec crouched down next to Ritchie Kelly, an Australian soldier who said "We're surrounded in the worst kind of way. Our Captain got killed yesterday just trying to run and get some food. 18 bullets in him. These Japs shoot at you from six sides at once. The bastards swarm you like bees. We had the chance to evacuate, but someone back in England told us that we are in a strong position!"

He smiled at them as a bullet whizzed past them, hitting a mule and it fell to the ground screaming. It was in so much pain, one of the Aussie soldiers took pity on it and put a bayonet into its neck.

Almost immediately a couple of young Malaysian boys ran out and started dragging it away. They'd eat well that night.

They were in the outer suburbs of a town and living like rats, hiding in nooks and crannies so the snipers could not pick them off.

Ted had been there less than an hour when news filtered through that the Japanese had landed on the West Coast of the island of Singapore and in less than a day, had pushed on almost fifty miles.

Alec had found a huge lump of wood and had put his helmet on it and kept bobbing it up and down over the wall he was hidden behind. Bullets would whizz by, never once hitting it. "Couldn't hit a barn door, Ted, we'll be alright with this lot!" They giggled and opened their rations, wondering why they had not had any orders to find a billet to sleep. They had been marching all day and a few lads were showing signs of malaria. The tablets they had been given were less than effective. Alec and Ted both had experience of fighting the German's, but had no clue about fighting the Japanese.

Word then came back to them that Captain Aitken was dead. The bullet wound had not been too severe, but as they operated on him in a building in the interior, three mortars had hit the hospital, killing three Malaysian nurses and eight patients, including Aitken.

The following morning there were more landings at Muar, with the enemy using custom built landing craft that did not just stop at the beach but could drive along the sand making sure it was safe to let off the soldiers inside.

Once again, Alec was up to his old tricks. He had sneaked out to the kitchens and stolen some fruit. He gave Ted some green looking thing. He had no clue as to what it was, but ate it anyway.

A new Australian Officer appeared and took charge. His name was Reay and he seemed to know what he was doing. He had just returned from a patrol where only he and 24 Australians had attacked a bicycle patrol of thirty Japanese, wiping them out without a single wounding to his men.

Ted was surrounded by Aussies and was trading cigarettes for chocolate when he was told that three days before he arrived, they had evacuated all civilians from a mile wide strip of land in the north of the island. The Australians had heard how the Japanese had attacked islands belonging to their country. The most common moan was 'Why are we here when they could be landing in Australia next.'

In Parliament, the Australian Prime Minister, Mr Curtin had gone so far as to say "For the first time in the countries history, Australian territory has been attacked. The enemies next stroke could even be to attempt the mainland itself. We are ready!"

"Some bloody Fortress this is," said Alec returning from the latrine, a haphazard trench dug behind some buildings. "Near got killed by a pig!"

He explained how he was just sitting down when a wild pig had wandered in by accident, got a shock and charged at him. With his shorts around his ankles, he couldn't get out of the way so was pushed backwards and his right boot had gone into the river of shite. Ted chastised him for letting the pig get away, "I could murder a bacon sandwich."

He spent the next hour or so trying to clean his boot and wash his sock.

That night they were playing cards in bright moonlight and Ted had won all kinds of stuff; a chain and a cross, some biscuits and a Japanese flag. He'd even got a few quid off Alec who had taken the huff and stopped playing after being wiped out after only a few games.

There had been no attacks and it was the quietest of their five nights there.

They had no idea that what was about to occur would change their lives forever.

Chapter 3

For some reason, Ted woke early on the morning of February 15th, 1942.

It was around 6.30am and yet officers were rushing around in all directions, while the bulk of the defending force slept at their posts. It seems that Lieutenant General Percival had met with the Japanese under a flag of truce in the Ford Works on Bukit Timah Hill.

Churchill broadcast that the fortress island of Singapore had fallen before the soldiers on the ground knew. He said to the world "Here is the moment to display calm and poise, combined with grim determination, which not so very long ago brought us out of the very jaws of death!"

Knowing that the island was the only major dry dock between Durban and Pearl Harbour, this was a significant victory for Japan. They blew up the Johor Causeway so no one could escape. The waking troops were surprised to see a white flag raised above the camp.

The officers had gathered everyone together to explain that they had surrendered to the enemy and they had to lay down their arms. The furore that followed was a mixture of anger and fear, men who had watched their friends killed to defend the island roared their disapproval in no uncertain terms. One asked a very salient question "Why were we not allowed to evacuate back to Australia?" At least then they could defend their homes. The British contingent, who had only gone in there days before, were at a loss to the genius who told them to reinforce a place that another officer had already agreed to give up.

From the tree-line opposite the British defensive position, there was movement, around three or four hundred Japanese soldiers tentatively moving toward them.

Ted heard Alec shout "Oh my God; they're coming... do we shoot them? Do we run... what are we supposed to do?"

The Australian Officer Reay shouted, "Hold your ground, place your weapons on the floor and do not resist. They will uphold the Geneva Convention so you'll be looked after till the end of this bloody war!"

The Japanese soldiers came amongst them, placing weapons onto long carts and pushing the men into the central area. Reay tried to act as a route of communication, yet the Japanese didn't care. One slapped him across the face with a wooden stick. The Japanese were going through the pockets and kit bags of each soldier.

In the fourth tier, Alec started frantically groping around Ted's bag and dragged from it the Japanese flag, scrunching it up into a ball and throwing it into the bushes. Ted wrote "If I had been found with that, they would have killed me on the spot. It would have made them think I had taken it from a dead officer rather than won it in a poker game. Once again Alec had saved my life."

Within six weeks a massive prisoner of war camp had been opened called Changi, with smaller camps being erected like satellites around it. The dead had all been buried and relative calm had descended. The food was miserable - a corn soup with very little corn. It certainly was not enough to give a man strength.

It was around this time that the camp heard of three major atrocities. First, a group of 17 western nurses had been dragged from a hospital, gang-raped and then bayoneted to death. Their bodies had been found piled up in the jungle, having been thrown away like rubbish. Then, at the Alexander Hospital, rather than care for the sick the Japanese had bayoneted them all. As the doctors and nurses tried to defend and protect their patients they were massacred in a hail of machine gun fire.

It wasn't just the military who suffered. Almost every young woman in Singapore was raped by the soldiers. Any who protested would be killed, often along with their families. The atrocities were too numerous to be a coincidence. It became apparent to Ted that he was in a precarious hell that he would most likely not survive.

No sooner had he thought that when two Japanese dragged a soldier into the camp, kicked open the door to the hut and threw the broken body onto the floor. With a massive waft of dust, his head hit the wood and began to bleed. The man was Eddie Warton from the Suffolk Regiment and to everyone's surprise, he sat up, swore and asked for a fag.

After some weak tea made without any tea and a dried biscuit, there was colour back in his cheeks. Ted and Alec were from the Suffolk Regiment and had been supposed to join the Suffolk's already there but had never found them. At first, they had joined the Border Regiment, but during their training, a group of them were given to the Suffolk's who had been caught very short handed.

Thirty-eight Scots and North Easterners found themselves the butt of a thousand jokes because of their accents. Ted wondered where his other mates in the Border Regiment where now. In fact, they were fighting in Italy but doing much better than he was. Suddenly there were whistles, a signal to run outside and stand to attention. This, most did, despite cankers, boils, sores, dysentery and malaria. Those that were slow were beaten with rifle butts and on some occasions, killed with bayonets. This gave everyone enough incentive to get there on time.

A Japanese Officer stood in front of them shouting as a soldier translated "A pistol has been stolen from a Japanese soldier. It will be returned or some of you will die."

It was about 11.20am and the temperature was 95 degrees. Everyone stood there for four hours in the severe sun until one man came forward and said that the person who had the gun had escaped. The Officer asked him why he had not reported the escape. The young soldier, a corporal, said "It is our duty as prisoners of war to try to escape."

At that, the Officer drew his pistol and barked something. The translator said "For every man who escapes, three will die."

He was about to shoot the corporal when another officer stepped forward and whispered something to him. He laughed and ordered his men to take the corporal and two other men outside the camp. Across the field, there was a wooden hut used as the officer's quarters, next to that a canteen and about eighty yards further away, a latrine. It seems the canteen had been overrun by huge red ants and the only way that they could stop them infesting the kitchens was to throw the food waste into pits so they went for that instead.

The three soldiers had their hands and legs tied and two pieces of wood were placed across the waste trench. One on the prisoner's chin, the other at the back of the neck and so

11

they could not slide along. Belts were then used to secure the pieces of wood together.

Daily, the other prisoners watched as these three blokes were eaten alive while starving to death. They screamed for almost four days until the fight had gone from them and the ants could make their way up the nose into the skull, through the ear to enter the eardrum, down the throat and into any open wounds on their poor battered bodies.

The other prisoners could not sleep hearing those screams without wondering who would be next.

Chapter 4

One of the first things that Ted discovered was that days and nights all blur into one.

This was also when Ted and Alec suffered something that was unpleasant and all too common. It was a blight known as Changi balls.

For some reason, everyone had severe pain in their testicles and their medical officer confirmed it was due to poor nutrition, shocking hygiene and the lice and tics that everyone had no choice but to suffer. Alec told the M.Q. that he had been scratching all night long to such a degree that his testicles were red raw and bleeding. He spent the night picking off the bugs that seemed to feed on those open wounds.

Ernest Warwick was also there and he wrote:

"My mate Dill told me he had a cure for Changi balls. He said if any of us ever expect to get out of this hell hole we have to look after our chopper and balls. The Aussies were desperate to find out how to end that misery because everyone was being driven crazy. The answer was tea. Cold bleeding tea. You get your mess tin; half fill it with cold tea,

13

then sit and dangle your cobblers in it for half an hour. At first, the lads thought it was so unlikely, but the sensation you got was amazing. It's a feeling of utter relief. Almost like some bird stroking them with cold fingers. Don't know how it works, but its bleeding beautiful!"

Alec was soon soaking his balls in copious amounts of tea that an Australian lad was trading.

One night after a long day rebuilding walls for a new workhouse, Ted returned to the hut to find 18 of the lads all soaking their privates that way. "Well that's not something you see every day" he chuckled, yet within five minutes he had joined them!

As soon as their work detail ended, night fell like a net. One moment it was light, the next pitch black.

They were now at a camp called Ban Pong. The cama-raderie was incredible, people you had just met you treated like a lifelong friend. The only problem was that life there would usually not last as long as lives anywhere else. Alec said that he had left a packet of salt next to the water butt in the square and was about to nip out to get it. The problem was there was a curfew and severe punishments were dished out to any transgressor. A young British lad, barely 18, called Thomas said "I'll sneak and get it for you."

This was commonly done, most folks having moved from hut to hut unseen, so Alec thought nothing of it. However, after about three minutes there was a cry and the lads raced to the window where they saw the young lad panicking and running. There were two shots and the back of his head exploded before he fell onto the wooden steps at the front of their hut. The ragged uniform confirmed who it was, but what was left of his face was unrecognisable. A Japanese officer marched into the square with two soldiers holding one leg each as they dragged him outside the encampment. The dead body was unceremoniously dumped on the red ant's nest, next to the three skeletal bodies of those other poor souls.

The Japanese were talking about building a railway and some British soldiers with engineering experience were forced to help them.

Not long after, whispers went right around the camp that two Aussie soldiers called Murray and Goodwin had decided to escape.

Taking their chance to get as far away from the enemy as possible, their plan was simple: the latrine trench, affectionately known as 'shit-track alley', went under the wire as the Japanese had a slightly more sophisticated one further up. They planned to use two hollowed out pieces of bamboo and slide under the hundreds of gallons of excreta and move slowly through to the Japanese side late in the evening, then slip out and run off into the jungle mere thirty yards away.

Not a great plan but plausible.

What they underestimated was the horror of that shit pit. The trench stretched for about ten feet on the prisoner side and ten more of the Japanese side. It was three and a half feet wide and between eight and ten feet deep in places. What this meant was that you could never rest your feet on the bottom. The surface of the pit was covered entirely with juicy fat maggots and swarming with every species of fly known to man. At about eight, Goodwin broke curfew and sneaked into the latrine. Lowering his body into the moving mass of insects, he dragged himself along the side of the trench, ducking under the wire into the Japanese side.

There was no going back.

Murray would have followed, but couldn't face the idea of climbing into that crawling, buzzing pit. This left poor Goodwin with the decision to go it alone.

Just as he sought to climb out on the enemy side, a soldier walked past and found him. He called for more soldiers to come, yet none wanted to drag him out of there.

Finally, they decided to bayonet his arms so that he sank into the pit. He tried bravely to use his feet to keep his head out of that stinking mire, but after about ten minutes or so he couldn't anymore and sank into the crap. The Japanese were roaring with laughter and two of them sat on the wooden shelf, emptying their bowels to celebrate his death.

The following morning every man in Ted's hut was ordered to put their boots on as they were going on a forced march. There were two Captains due to supervise the men, Seaton and Hill. Both were decent but very much upper class, yet their men were obsessively loyal.

To march thirty or so miles a day wearing boots without socks, with blisters the size of goose eggs was no walk in the park. Any man who faltered had to be carried or the Japanese Officer Usaka would shoot them.

On that road, they buried four men, one from a heart attack, one from exhaustion and two shot dead for backchat. They were dumped in shallow graves by the roadside.

Later that day, seemingly angered by the brutality and murder, Captain Hill had demanded a meeting with Usaka. During that meeting, he had pointed out to him that after the war, they would track him down as a war criminal unless he started to treat his prisoners in an honourable fashion. To question the honour of a Japanese officer was utterly unacceptable.

Hill was killed.

One soldier, Shepherd, claimed to witness it. A resident of Low Fell in Gateshead, he wrote after the war:

"He was a gentle and obviously educated man, Captain Hill. He did what he could, asking for food and medical supplies, then he mentioned a lack of honour and it all kicked off. The Japanese officer snatched a rifle from a guard, one with a bayonet on it and he stuck it in the Captain's gut, twirling it about and tearing out all of his innards. They were bursting out through his bloody vest. Then yards of his intestines just flopped onto the floor. He toppled forward to the floor, all the while insulting this murderous swine. Once he was on the floor, the officer drew a small dagger and slashed the back of his neck, I guess cutting his spinal cord. It was an awful thing. I was ordered back to the rest of the boys. Next morning, the bugle let everyone know he had gone."

The next day they were trudging again through the dusty, dirty and winding hillside tracks of the fever-ridden jungles of Thailand.

As they marched, the medical officers insisted that everyone sang 'She'll be Coming round the Mountain when she Comes'. It was a simple technique to keep up morale but seemed to work.

After walking for what felt like forever, they were huddled under trees for another night out in the open. Just then, there was an explosion from one of the tents housing the Japanese. A group of four had been playing cards using an ammunition box as a table and the lamp had fallen, sending the burning oil into the case where it exploded. This, in turn, fired shells in all directions like firecrackers.

At first, they thought they were under attack, but on realising that they had killed some of their own, the spirits of the Allies soared. Chat began, discussing all the things they were missing; egg and chips, roast beef and Yorkshire puddings, sausages and then conversation turned to their sweethearts. Alec said "What I wouldn't give for a bunk up with my wife right now... guaranteed there would be another kiddie on the way!"

Everyone laughed and the following morning as they marched past the site of the explosion, small pieces of flesh were splattered across the road and trees, being fed on by insects and monkeys.

Marching, marching, marching and every night, fewer of them left.

Death from pneumonia, another from extreme dehydration caused by dysentery, one made a run for it and was shot. Every single day it was a catalogue of misery. All they ate was a tiny amount of rice and anything they could snatch from the jungle in passing.

As the long column of prisoners trudged on, you could see a cloud of mosquitos, flies and even butterflies around them, drinking their blood, or waiting for them to die.

This was no paradise.

The other senior officer had decided it was time to speak out; he was smashed in the face with the butt of a rifle, shattering his teeth. As he cried out, a whoop of chattering monkeys began to howl from the trees.

A Scot named Willie Cochran decided he had taken enough. He had studied maps of Singapore and Thailand before he sailed out and was confident he recognised the mountainous region to the right of us. He thought he could get away to a place of safety and sounded out all of the lads. They all wanted to go but were fatigued and sick, so Willie decided to go it alone.

He was a lithe, skinny bloke, only about 5 feet 5 inches tall. During the night, he crawled off into the jungle as some of the Australians orchestrated a fight as a diversion.

Halfway through the usual, uncomfortable nights sleep, Ted awoke upon hearing a scream but drifted back into unconsciousness.

The following morning the Japanese stood us all at attention and said "In future, if anyone escapes, ten men will be taken out and shot."

At first, everyone wanted to cheer believing Willie had made it until four soldiers dragged in a snake that had to be 25 feet long. There, in the middle, was an enormous, man-sized bulge.

In broken English, an attendant to the Japanese captain said "It seems that English soldiers are good to eat!" and laughed. They pushed the snake back into the brush and marched us away again.

Every day there were enough stories to fill a book. Lives of good men lost.

They had no choice but to keep going and concentrate on keeping themselves and their friends alive.

Most would not make it home.

Chapter 5

I t must have been surreal for the lads from places like Durham, Gateshead, Edinburgh and Merseyside to find themselves in a jungle clearing, watching elephants move huge trees about as the survivors finished planning to build a huge bridge.

At this point, something unexpected happened. A group of Thai's were often used to prepare the food while thousands of them were being used as slave labour. Imagine the sexual tension when Thai women were cooking and washing the pots surrounded by hundreds of sex-starved prisoners.

It was evident from the demeanour of the Japanese that they were using these women and that angered the Allied troops who all, deep down, wanted sex just as badly. On one occasion, a lad from Southport tried to rape a young Thai girl and upon being captured the Japanese shot them both.

Other Thai's were trying to help the prisoners, many of them starving, their bodies covered in boils, bites and sores. They would sneak some of the medical supplies to senior officers who would share them out.

The situation with boils was horrid. The only way to stop them becoming infected was to cut open the huge lump and have one of your mates suck out the pus and spit it out. Remembering that some had boils deep around their anus, under arms, on the penis, feet and thighs, it was a humiliating and disgusting practice.

However, it saved many a life from septicaemia.

It was at this point that the lads met a Japanese officer they would come to know as Doctor Death. The officer, who spoke excellent English, would establish who was fit enough to work on the fledgeling bridge. His real name was Major Toyota. That morning, the parade was full of the walking dead with some completely unable to walk. If a man complained of leg ulcers, the 'Doctor' would simply get out a scalpel and cut it out, throw some salt on the open wound and send the man off to work.

This one particular day, a man named Alfie Andrews from Liverpool turned up with 56 boils on his body. One on his nose had completely closed his eye.

The doctor looked at him and whispered something to an orderly who took him away. They never saw him again.

Most men had the runs and those too weak to work were given a warning. If they had not recovered enough to work the following day they would be killed. Food was too scarce to waste on dying men.

By this time a group of American prisoners had arrived, upsetting the flow of things.

The Japanese told the newcomers that British officers were in charge and they had to help. The Americans, unaware of the brutality of their captors, tried it on. Refusing to work, demanding more food and medical supplies, a young Captain Downey decided to speak out.

The next day at roll call he was found hanged in the centre of camp next to the flag pole. The Japanese flag, the rising sun, was raised. After this, though the Americans were still verbal, they were a damn sight more careful.

Ted and Alec kept their heads down, but were getting to know who the most dangerous and likely to kill you were. Lieutenant Takasaki was known as 'The Rat' because he stuck his nose everywhere. He discovered a lot of black market stuff and they loathed him for it.

Sergeant Noro known as 'Baldy' was a vicious beast who had beaten a few prisoners to death, but the worst was Sergeant Yamamoto 'The Fig', who raped the Thai girls repeatedly. There were tales that he had also buggered some of the younger male prisoners. His right-hand man was a soldier called Yoshi who just wanted to please his boss and would kill a man who even looked at him the wrong way.

One evening a group of local village girls had been dragged to the camp to 'entertain' the soldiers. Some of the girls were about 11 or 12 years old and they were about to be raped by a few dozen men each.

Ted, Alec and 'Sandy' Beech were watching from a distance. Alec said "For fuck's sake, they're babies! My daughters not that much younger than that little one!"

As they stared out towards the soldiers' billets, there was one little girl of around seven years old. Corporal 'Dekka' Haynes shouted some obscenity towards the soldiers who were throwing these children around.

Three gunshots rattled towards us hammering into trees. The soldiers were selecting their victims, and Yoshi dragged this little tiny girl into his tent. The girls had been warned that if they did not 'please' their partner, they would be killed along with their entire families.

Yet this tiny little child just screamed and screamed and screamed. Such was the agony and indignity that she suffered. After a while, Yoshi stepped out of his tent bare-chested as if to show the world what he had done.

There was no remorse or guilt. He looked like the cat that had gotten the cream. The child couldn't walk and blood dripped down her naked thighs. She was shaking and sobbing as the next soldier dragged her into his tent laughing.

Hundreds of British, American and Australian soldiers had watched the horror unfolding before them and done nothing but disapprove. They were all ashamed.

Then, three Thai men who had been minding the elephants walked up to the tent with the young girl. They crept in and came out with her, one running off with her under his arm into the relevant safety of the jungle while the other two walked to Yoshi's tent. They knocked on the post and he stepped out, still smiling smugly but irritated he had been disturbed.

Before he could speak, he was hit hard with a machete across the head and fell to his knees. The blade had sliced into his skull at an angle from his left eyebrow down to the corner of his mouth. The Thai men ran towards the trees and vanished. The Allied troops were beginning to cheer, but were quietened down by their officers. Alec said, "That's the ballsiest thing I've ever seen!"

Ted shook his head "There'll be hell to pay now though."

Once the bodies were found, Hell did visit Tonchan Camp.

The soldiers were ordered out with the innocent Thai

girls; they were all asked who was responsible. Apparently, they had no idea. They were beaten with bayonets, but still could not answer, so Yamamoto shot one young girl in the head. Again, they could not answer a question they did not know the answer to, so they were bayoneted to death. The Allies roared out boo's, but a volley of shots quietened them down.

Next morning, the blood was everywhere and there in the corner of the camp was a pile of dead children. Ted and the boys had to walk over the very patch of ground where they had been murdered. Insects were feeding on the bodies and you could see the haze of bugs surrounding the corpses in the distance.

As they queued in the blood pool, one American could not hold his tongue, "You fucking monsters…"

He never finished his sentence. Instead, he was beaten with pickaxe handles by two guards and dragged into the jungle. There was a single shot.

Ted looked at Alec; it was a look of 'lets do something'. Instead, Alec grabbed his friend by the arm.

"Ted, we are going to get out of here. My family need me and I'm not going to let you throw your life away!"

Ted had Nora at home, his fiancée of three years. "They stop you feeling like a man Alec. We're supposed to fight these buggers."

Alec nodded "We'll fight them any way we can, but suicide would be stupid."

At that moment, a Thai man was dragged into the heart of the camp. He was not one of the brave men who rescued the little girl, most likely just walking along minding his business.

The soldiers mobbed him, beating him with rifle butts, jabbing him with bayonets, stamping and kicking him. An order was then given to dump the body on top of those of the poor girls.

As they looked at those bloodied bodies, lifeless eyes stared back.

Ted began to cry.

Chapter 6

I magine living each day without knowing what day it was, never sure what month it was or if one year was ending and another beginning.

Such was the severity of their fragile lives; the only focus was survival.

Imagine if one morning came and you knew something was very wrong. Well, at 4 am there was a scream and Ginger Slatoe started writhing in agony. His barrack mates tried to stifle his screams knowing that the swiftest way the Japanese guards knew of curing an ill was with a bayonet or machete. He told everyone he thought he had another kidney stone and he needed painkillers.

They scattered around the barracks and came up with nothing except a tiny phial of rice wine, nothing close to coping with that type of pain. So they had no choice but to stand at the door of their hut and attract the attention of the guards. This carried great risk. Another hut who had done this had been forced to stand out in the sun for eight hours until every single man had collapsed.

Ted, Alec and Sandy carried Ginger, all the time

screeching his discomfort. The guards allowed him to be taken to the hospital.

It was a hospital only in the loosest of terms. A stinking, large bamboo hut where doctors, nurses and orderlies worked ten-hour shifts trying to keep the prisoners alive so they could work for their Japanese masters.

Some patients were shaking uncontrollably, suffering from dysentery, others coughed and spat long phlegm-like globules onto the bed and floor, sometimes dripping it down their chin and chests.

The ward was alive with retching, farting and pleas for help. The sheets were stained with other peoples shit, urine and blood, yet they were only allowed to wash them once a week, so disease and infections were rife.

The orderly, usually some pale-faced, stick-thin prisoner, had to scoop up the faeces, wipe the stain with antiseptic and then rest the patient back down on it. The stink of vomit was in everything and although some of the Japanese medics wore masks, most of the workers just had to breathe it in, often causing them throw up too.

It was normal to hear someone begging for an arm or a leg to be amputated, so bad was the pain of septicaemia. Others obviously had gangrene in wounds, that mouldy green look and telltale smell giving it away.

The lads offered to help make Slatoe comfortable, mopping floors and emptying buckets of blood and dressings into a midden outside. Upon emptying his first pail, Ted looked into the hole to see it had at least three dead soldiers in it, along with an amputated leg, a hand and what seemed like a mountain of entrails.

There were a dozen or so rats down there, feasting on what was becoming a human buffet. He got a bit of a shock when a rat, irritated by his appearance, had ran at him with its teeth bared. He kicked it hard back into the pit.

An orderly called Munro had suffered kidney stones in the past, so took pity on Slatoe. He got him a little medication and forced him to drink about half a gallon of warm rice water.

Munro asked him to look away. Slatoe, who was still contorted in agony, thought he was going to get an injection. Instead, the orderly hit him with a wooden block behind the ear, knocking him unconscious.

Kindest thing he could do for Slatoe at the time. The friends worked all night in the hospital, despite having been clearing away the jungle all day. They knew if you left someone there, they rarely returned. At 6.30 they tried to wake Slatoe up, ready for roll call. They all made it in time and were assigned their work for the day.

Once again they were to clear the jungle for the railway tracks.

That day, each prisoner was given a card that read '**IMPERIAL JAPANESE ARMY**'. On the other side it read, '**I, a Japanese prisoner of war, I am very happy. I work for my pay. I am not in the hospital and I am very well treated, Signed…**'

Every prisoner had to sign it, the only man refusing an American called Peter McIntosh.

He shouted to the other Yanks "All it takes is one person and then they have to treat us right. They're reckoning we'll prosecute them like the fucking war criminals they are! Guys, we are not signing!"

Very brave, but he was immediately dragged away by a

Japanese guard and a group of about 8 Thai workers were ordered to kill him, or they would be machine gunned. He was hacked to death behind the hospital and his body thrown into that stinking midden. The Americans were forced to sign by their commanding officer.

The camp was starving.

Most of the men were half dead and now lying to cover their captor's atrocities. During that day Ginger was ill, but they managed to hide it from the guards well enough. Then on returning, they took him back to the hospital.

Timing in life is always vital and the lads timed it completely wrong. As they arrived at the hospital door, Doctor Death sounded off at the Japanese doctors. It seemed that the work was not going quickly enough and they needed more men. The hospital was not fixing them up fast enough. The British and American doctors helped explain that if they were fed the men better, they would recover quicker.

Doctor Death paid no attention and ordered half the patients back to work the following day or there were to be serious repercussions. Everyone had heard of another camp hospital where patients were murdered for 'refusing to work'. Three had had legs amputated that day and a dozen or so were in agony with a range of life-threatening infections.

It made no difference and gave such incentive to those that could walk to get out and work themselves to death rather than getting a bullet to the head.

To everyone's surprise, British and American engineers were getting things done, the bridge foundations beginning to shape up. Some of the British lads called them traitors as they got better rations, clean uniforms and light work duties. Ted was more philosophical "If we've got to be here, make it easier for yourself any way you can!"

They managed to get Slatoe back to the hut where they gave him bottled urine to drink. It was the only liquid they had a decent amount of. He would gag while drinking the warm piss that each man had been ordered to keep. Two days later, he passed the kidney stone and was back to decent health. His only problems from that day were the thousands of 'pissy breath' insults he received.

Just then four Japanese slammed into the barracks and ordered everyone out. The men had just completed a 14-hour shift in the jungle and had expected to fall into a deep sleep. Instead under the floodlights, they were standing to attention as Major Aiki ordered one of his men to translate.

A Colonel from the Australian army and British Officer Ashdown had been caught operating a radio set. None of the lads in Ted's barrack had a clue they had one. It seems an Australian lad had been tortured and the only information he had was regarding the radio. His finger and toenails had been jabbed with bamboo before being torn out with pliers. Three of his fingers on his right hand had been cut off and his eyes gouged out.

Very few men would not have talked.

As they dragged him out to return him to his barracks, Aiki pulled out his pistol and shot him in the back of the head. The translator said "The major knows that is how you treat traitors."

Poor young lad looked no more than 18 years old.

Then the translator declared "We intend to make an example of the prisoners. We are the master race! You must obey or death can be swift, as you have seen. If you disobey, death can be very slow."

At that moment two of the Japanese guards stripped two

men to the waist and forced them to move forwards. The two officers were trying hard to remain at full attention, but you could see their knees trembling. Both were married with young families and were decent men. The men loved them, but as they stared past them, four huge machine guns were pointed into the ranks, ready if they were to try and stop anything that might be about to happen.

Officer Ashdown spoke out. "Stand down men; this is one we must pay for. Stay alive. That is my only order!"

The Australian Colonel shouted "Its been my honour… and our time is coming!" He was about to say something else when one of the guards armed with a pickaxe handle knocked him to his knees. Then he began beating his feet. The other got stuck into Ashdown and they both began to scream in agony.

The guards had been ordered to break every bone in their bodies whilst keeping them alive as long as possible. First, the feet and toes became mulch, bones poking out of the mashed skin. Then they move onto the ankles, legs, knees, thighs before hammering over and over on their hips until the other prisoners could hear them shattering.

The two officers could do nothing. Their arms and hands were then broken. One of the guards picked up the colonel's head to show him his broken, ragdoll body then dropped it down, beginning to break one rib after another.

The colonel's mouth was dripping and frothing with blood.

By this time, Ashdown was already dead. Both guards began hammering over and over on the men's faces until they were unrecognisable.

Amazingly, the Aussie colonel was still alive and moaning audibly.

Major Aiki did not like that and started slapping the guard

who then began stamping on the man's shattered windpipe. He then bent down and began tearing at the man's tongue, yanking it through the flesh of his open throat.

Finally, with both men not just dead but splintered, they looked at the ranks of Allies, many desperate to meater out revenge.

Many had vomited, others were crying.

It was carnage.

The Japanese just stood there.

Chapter 7

I t was yet another dark day in the camp as word filtered through that thousands more prisoners were coming to the area to work on the railway.

That meant two things.

Firstly, the war could not be going well and secondly, all the sick and ailing prisoners would be put down like dogs and the others would have to do their work.

The lads were all instructed to get ready for a long march to meet all the Japanese officers who were travelling along the river by barge. As the tramped along the river, they passed what seemed like a never-ending row of prisoner of war camps. Each one having only one thing in common. Skeletal men in khaki staring back at us.

To talk about a march makes it sound a very straightforward affair. In reality it meant men with bleeding feet wobbling, trailing behind, getting kicked and beaten, stuck with a bayonet or getting a bullet.

The men did their best to support each other, but some were too weak to cope with the midday sun, day in and day out. Their skin hardened and leathery, their spirit strong but their poor bodies battered, they would sway and stagger until they saw the wooden camp they would soon call their new home.

100 kilometres from Tonchan, they arrived at Camp Tamajao. It looked very much like Tonchan, except it was built entirely of wood.

Three good men were lost on that march. One died seemingly of a heart attack and the other two were killed with a bayonet for wanting to carry the body of their friend with them. Everyone knew it was a stupid way to lose your life, yet some of the boys had just had enough.

Word came through that one POW's had grabbed a Japanese soldier's rifle, shot a machine gunner on the wall, disembowelled him and then walked up to the gate, shooting at anyone he could see. Then when the bullets ran out, he tried to get through to attack as many as he could with the bayonet. Upon realising he couldn't get through, he simply stood there waiting to be shot or captured.

As a crowd of guards raced toward the gate, the crazed soldier realised that this would probably mean the loss of his head. He certainly didn't want that, so instead took the bayonet of his captured weapon and placed the blade under his chin and using both hands, jerked it up through his skull and into his brain. He fell like a rag doll onto the parade ground.

The fact that he was dead didn't change the anger of the Japanese ,who had lost three of their number with a few others wounded. They jabbed him, stamped on him and kicked him around for a good fifteen minutes. It was later discovered that the man had been the camp pastor who had reached the end of his tether.

The busiest building in the new Tamajao camp was the hospital. Our new doctor Major Williams spent his life up to his elbows in blood. The gentle, rather portly chap was operating on poor helpless souls without anaesthetic, including the amputation of arms and legs.

While the lads were being put into huts, Ted and Alec found Ginger with some blokes that had been there a while. They stood in the blazing heat discussing what had been happening at the camp before they arrived. Their new comrades were Chas, Tommy, Jack and Bill. They seemed a decent bunch.

Chas was a rather outspoken cockney, Tommy was a welder from Sunderland, Jack was a rather posh older man and Bill, a smiling scot who was in the Australian army having moved from Perth Scotland to Perth Australia.

Despite their lengthy march, they were lectured about the standard of their work on the bridge. It was nearing completion and yet a train had neared the end of the current line before the embankment had fallen away. Had the train been going at any speed it would have fallen down the mountainside.

They were told the 48-man work detail had been punished. In fact, the new lads in the camp were taking their place. Two days later, a native hut was found full to the ceiling with the bodies of those unfortunate men, hacked into pieces.

Alec was one of the prisoners who found the bodies.

Ted wrote:

'He came back to the hut and ran to the window where he puked and puked. He told me that you could not tell where one body ended and another began. He said that he heard a voice in the middle of the heap begging for help. He couldn't see who it was and did not want any guard finding him there. The voice kept saying "Kill me... please, kill me... that rats are eating me alive... please god..."

It was a whisper Alec could never shake free of it.

He tried to claw his way into that bloody pile and realised a few of them were still alive. Others had heads missing or were ripped wide open.

The whispered voice seemed closer and he saw a hand move, so grabbed hold of it and tugged at it before falling over backwards - the arm had been hacked off.

To his credit, he kept digging in that bloody hill of bodies and finally found the bloke and yanked him to the edge of the heap.

The man was cut from the chin all the way down to the groin and his insides were still a few yards under the bodies where rats were racing around. You could clearly see his right leg was missing. The worst thing was that Alec said he was smiling and begging to be killed.

In that whisper, he said "Hit me with a rock... finish me off... please... don't let those rats get me... please... do it"

Alec looked around for a stone that would suit his purpose but just as he picked it up, a guard walked in and kicked him over. He ordered him back to the work detail.

Alec stared at the soldier; the guard looked back at him, spat and walked off, laughing. As Alec was chased back to work, he heard the whispering voice disappear.

It stayed with him from that day on.

In Tamajao 241 nearby, a young lad about 20 suffering from severe leg ulcers, hobbled towards one of the enormous camo bonfires and to the horror of all his friends threw himself into the middle of it to die.

Stories like this were becoming common. It was hard to believe, but things were about to get worse. The bridge was coming on well, yet it was never good enough for the Japanese who continually forced the pace. The fact it was being built at all was a miracle amidst pretty non-stop rain.

The monsoon season was firmly upon them. Still, the elephants were moving massive beams and the entire site was in full swing. Working on top of the bridge was a slippery business; numerous men had fallen to their deaths. The soldiers did anything they could to make sport. One stood next to a blacksmith heating up the rivets for laying track. He would flick these white hot things down the two hundred feet or so and kill a few people.

Another lad got one down his shirt and it burned right into his stomach. He lasted a few days. Behind Ted's work area he saw some Koreans who worked with the Japanese, digging a huge grave pit. Once exhumed, the bodies of the dead that scattered the work area were removed and thrown in unceremoniously.

Some of the dead had been lying in the stream for a few days and were bloated with gas. One, a corporal, was being carried by two prisoners to the pit when he exploded. Everyone was covered in blood and guts including a Japanese officer who thought it was less than funny. He fired a shot at one lad who laughed.

"Speedo" shouted the officer and everyone hurried to get what was left of the stinking bodies to the freshly dug pit. Then prisoners were ordered to carry men who were still alive to the pit. These poor men, who were sick and incapable of putting a shift in, couldn't even struggle to their feet. At first, the men tried to argue but were beaten until they did as they were told.

One of the men trying to plead for their life was Jack from our hut. The Abingdon lad was doing what he could, but had taken a rifle butt across the face and was bleeding.

Ted shouted, "Button it Jack, for God's sake. Shut yer mouth!"

It was too late. An officer with a knife sliced into the tendons behind both his knees and he crumpled to the ground.

They then dragged him to that pit, overloaded with the dead and dying and ordered the rest of the prisoners to fill it in. They all looked shocked, but two bullets wizzed past their heads and they began slowly scooping that dry soil onto the writhing mass of their comrades.

Jack shouted "Just do it, lads, I'm finished. Whatever happens. If you ever get home, tell my wife Elsie that my last ever thought was of her!" At that, one of the Koreans stepped forward and swung his shovel hard down onto his head. It burst like a ripe melon, covering everyone in his blood. Then they filled up that pit.

Ted whispered to the Korean and thanked him, for that was a mercy and poor Jack was fortunate not to have seen it coming.

No one was sure why so many men were dying. Yes, the food wasn't enough, the hygiene was rife and occasionally a poisonous snake would strike, but dozens were failing daily.

The next misery to attack these valiant men was about to make itself known.

Cholera.

Chapter 8

I t wasn't long before all of the camps were suffering with an outbreak of cholera.

The watery diarrhoea, stinking out the entire area, was quickly spread by the tainted water. Had it been adequately treated, few, if any, would have died. In that environment, it was lethal.

One entire hut was dead in less than a week. It seemed just to run and run and in less than two months, 1878 men had died of cholera alone. As soon as they were in the ground, even more prisoners would arrive.

It was a circle of death.

Still, some of the prisoners were trying to find ways to make mischief. One wrapped a fishing net around the propellers of a river barge. It appeared to be accidental, so no one died on the back of it. Two lads loaded gunpowder into the barges furnace so when it was next lit it exploded, killing three Thai natives; poor innocent men forced to work for their enemy. The men who did that were guilty of killing their own. However, Tommy Gill from Sunderland was involved in something that was a black eye to their Japanese hosts.

In the jungle about half a mile from the river, the Japanese had found a school with about thirty young children aged from about 5 to 10 and brought them into the camp.

Ted and the lads all waved and made faces and behaved like men do when children suddenly appear. What the Japanese soldiers would do to these beautiful little children was all too frightening to imagine. So Tommy asked the Americans to create a diversion and quite a distraction it was.

It was so beautifully done.

A large group of Yanks screamed that one leg of the bridge was going to collapse. If it did, the entire thing would come down. They all stood around the pillar and the engineer ordered ropes to secure it. All the while, the men on top were rushed to safety along with their guards. This would have been a disaster and the Japanese major would lose face, so it was vital that this be rectified.

While all eyes were on the panic, Tommy Gill and two Welshmen, Graham Davies and Dai Jones sneaked to the back of the hut where the children and old woman were housed. They dug a hole in the wall and helped them out. They then crept back into camp and draped a few scraps of cloth on trees pointing in the wrong direction of the most impenetrable jungle. The three men then crept back into camp. If they had escaped with the children, ten men would have been killed.

Six hours later, the wobbly leg of the bridge was supposedly stabilised and just as the guards were returning to their posts, there was a fire in the blacksmith's shop. Tommy thought the longer the guards were preoccupied, the more chance those tiny waifs would have.

Ted wrote:

"Tommy was a quiet bloke, but I take my hat off to him, if

it were not for him those children were finished. He took not one bit of credit for putting his life on the line. He was a proper man!"

The one thing that this adventure of Tommy's and the others had shown everyone was that you could escape.

The Japanese presumed the children had gotten themselves out, yet escape was now a distinct possibility, even if it cost ten lives.

Chapter 9

Every morning, the whispered news bulletins coming from Thai labourers told worse and worse news.

One day, we learned that 146 Thai workers had been found to be helping prisoners and all had been beheaded after being tortured by the Japanese version of the Kempi-Tai. Another day, they were told that the Allies had landed in Italy and were making headway.

Geordie Dunlop was, as the name suggested, from Newcastle and he used to talk so fast no one could understand him. Geordie inadvertently gave Chas Coxon, the hut's cockney, an idea. He explained that each evening the barge travelled down to a Thai village for supplies for the guards and to take some of them for 'companionship' with the working girls there.

Could a man get away without costing anyone their life? Ted wrote:

"We all wanted to escape, but none of us wanted to drop our mates in it. Chas was smart about it. It was our duty to dump our dead into a pit, so he had found a man that had died that day, dragged him into our barracks and put him in his bed. Then he crept out and managed to get down to the river unseen, slid into the water, roped himself to the barge and was hauled down into the Thai town. There, he found help to get himself hidden. We never saw nor heard from him again, but we know the Japanese never got him! Next morning on rising, we were all inconsolable that our 'Chas' had died in the night. The M.O. came in and his body was taken to the pit where it had come from. It was genius."

During the quiet celebration, Alec noticed that Ginger was missing. On glancing into the square, he spotted him tied up and being sliced by a Japanese guard. It seems he had failed to bow when an officer had walked by and being ordered to do so, had used a phrase involving the word 'oy'.

He had been severely beaten and his chest was covered with slashes from a knife. In the long years they had been there, they had lost hundreds of friends and thousands of comrades in arms, yet every single day was a battle for each man to stay alive.

The Siam-Burma Railway had led to some of the most inhumane atrocities of World War Two. Day by day there were the roars of bombers flying overhead as Allied planes bombed Bangkok to disrupt the Japanese in any way they could.

Alec, who had persuaded them to release Ginger, was putting what little salt they had onto his wounds. He was a mess and yet he looked at those planes saying "Imagine... just there above our heads are our lads, free... while we are in this Hell on Earth. Maybe they could spare us a bomb and get us out of our..."

"Stop that talk," said Alec, always one of those 'cup half full' people, "We've survived when so many have been lost.

Let's see it through, my darling is waiting for me. Those children will not recognise their own Dad, but we'll make up for lost time. You can come for tea, if you buck your ideas up."

Alec was a hero to everyone who knew him. He would put them first and everyone adored him for that. Most people in the Tamajao's had to look after number one.

Mercifully, these poor creatures had no idea that it would be almost another two full years before the war would be over for them.

Chapter 10

Beyond the blood-soaked jungles of Thailand, the American's were hammering the Japanese in some of the most devastating sea battles.

They had already recaptured the islands of Guam and Saipan and were getting closer to mainland Japan. The Emperor Hirohito had promised that no bombs would ever fall on Japan.

Soon the Allies would make him into a liar.

Many ships carried prisoners of war in their holds to try to deter LJS ships from trying to sink them. One such vessel was the Hotuku Maru, sunk on the 21st September 1944 by American bombers off the coast of Manila. In the hold had been 1300 British and Australian prisoners who had helped build the railway through Thailand.

Hirohito declared himself a God and went on the radio to say that he would one day rule the world.

The railway was now long since completed yet rotting away, the prisoners, many clinging on to life, left doing maintenance tasks.

Ginger had reached the point of wanting death, even yearning for it and one Tuesday he got it in a spectacular manner.

He was responsible for helping put water into trains from the water tower. He had chatted with his friends and said his goodbyes, while Alec had told him not to do anything stupid. The war was going well; now it was whether they could hold their nerve. A Korean, Kashito, had been on his case for the longest time and Ginger loathed him. So, as they stood on the train at the edge of the bridge, Ginger decided to act.

First, he slammed a massive lump of coal off the guard's head and then grabbed him, pushing his head against the red hot engine door, scalding the skin off his cheek. He then opened the furnace door and started pushing the wriggling but dazed Korean into the fire. He was burning and screaming, but his shrieks were covered by the flames and the steam off the water.

Ginger knew he was going to die, but his nemesis had paid for all he had done to so many. He climbed back up to the water hose, detached it and secured the lid before stepping off the train and walking along in front of it.

The Japanese soldiers shouted at him, one even fired at him, missing him by inches. He walked over to the edge, waved in the direction of his mates and as a bullet hit his shoulder he gave the guards a double V sign with his fingers. Then Ginger leapt out into nothing.

A perfect swan dive and he seemed to be in the air for the longest time before finally crashing into the rocky shallows.

Ted wrote:

"Alec, Tommy and I cried our eyes out because he was the fittest one of us. If he couldn't make it, what chance did the rest of us have? I have had dark thoughts. We are so sick of

46

the death around us all the time. I am ready to go. If I had a gun, I'd already been dead. Alec is the one who's kept us all going. He's so intent on raising those kids of his. He wants to see his wife and you know, I think he will. As for me, I'm not so confident."

Chapter 11

When one day feels like a month, the concept of years in a state of perpetual threat, seeing your friends die one by one, you start to forget what being human is.

Living becomes a terror of its own. How the spirits of brave men can be broken to such a degree that they yearn to surrender to death rather than spend another day under the cosh.

Every long, intolerable day was just as the day before, steeped in death and misery. The torture had become standard, being made to feel less than a man and not being able to make any decision as they were made for you. The mass brainwashing and humiliation of good men from India, Australia, America, Tibet and Britain.

It was apparent to all that things were changing. More Allied planes overhead, whispered stories of the bombing of all major Japanese cities. Then one morning Bill burst into the barracks and shouted "Well boys, it won't be long before you're home... I'll be in Perth discovering which one of those lucky Sheila's can have me!"

It was the latest whisper from a Thai native who had a hidden radio, risking his life daily to keep the prisoners up to date with the war. He had told them Hitler had died, that the Allies had rolled into Berlin, the Americans had won the battle of Midway and now that the Japanese Emperor was suing for peace. To all intents and purposes, the war was over. It could not have been better news. Now it was only a matter of time before they would all be free. They had made it! The sense of euphoria was tempered by the fact that as you walked into the square, you could see the bodies of the dead still being carried to the pits.

Bill was incredibly cocky. He stepped out and smiled at a guard, "Morning Smiler" he said, leaving the guard perplexed by it.

"Careful" Alec shouted, "We've not won yet. Don't give these bastards any excuse".

The war was over and yet in the jungles of Burma and Thailand, the British Fourteenth Army fought on regardless. The Japanese were on a full retreat, yet in hundreds of camps the torture, brutality and murder continued.

The Emperor had refused to give their prisoners the medical supplies provided by the Red Cross; hundreds continued to die every day of mistreatment, malnutrition and a swathe of different tropical diseases.

8th of May 1945 marked the official end of the war with Germany.

Winston Churchill warned that although there would be a short period for rejoicing, there was still the matter of Japan to deal with, as she remained unsubdued.

Back in Tokyo, the Emperor was told of the incredible

losses regarding men, equipment, ships, aircraft and the losses of vast areas of land he thought had been secured. Total defeat was not far away, primarily as the warlords who had demanded Japan go to war, were now all fighting amongst themselves. The prisoners had all been heartened by the news, yet could not understand why nothing had changed.

Ted wrote:

"We all sat around discussing what we would do when, not if, we got out of it alive. Bill declared he was going to track down every single Japanese guard from their camp and beat them to death. I knew what he meant… the amount of hate and contempt they had shown us. There had not been one single guard to have given an ounce of compassion or kindness. In fact, we rated the guards depending on if they would beat us or kill us. Alec and I just wanted to go home and see our families."

Just then they heard that Jock Wallace from the hut next door had died of starvation during the night. Two others in another hut were gone too. Alec stared out into the square, watching the human skeletons walking around aimlessly, doing jobs the Japanese had ordered like carrying rocks from one side of the camp to the other.

Tomorrow they would have to bring them back.

Still, they were alive.

Suddenly a siren sounded, a noise they had never heard before. Above them appeared a squadron of aircraft accompanied by a strange whistling noise. This was new and the prisoners raced out to stare up at the Allied planes only to see strings of bombs crashing across the distant hillside. They exploded and seemed to get nearer.

The bridge.

The symbol of their conquest of fear was being targeted. There was a sinking feeling in their stomachs. That bridge had cost thousands of lives, of friends, brothers, comrades and it could go with a single hit. Then came the additional worry that, if it did fall, the Japanese would have them rebuild it at another outrageous cost of lives.

A huge explosion rocked the area just beyond the wire, shrapnel, tons of rubble and earth spattering them. Bill saw a piece of shrapnel hit a guard, knocking on his back. Seizing the opportunity, he grabbed a rock and hit him hard in the windpipe to finish him off before staring out to the distance in the hope that it had not been witnessed.

Further away, another long string of bombs hit the bridge just near a tunnel on the northern section. The other explosions caused an avalanche of rocks which damaged another stretch of track.

Miraculously, the bridge held.

Then a string of bombs danced through the camp killing 23 men who had hid in their hut. In a second, pieces of them were scattered across the camp. One prisoner was killed when a head and shoulder belonging to one of his hut mates hit him so hard that both skulls exploded. Another bomb hit two Japanese huts including their main barracks.

Ironically it was empty.

There was only one plane left to make its run.

Alec spotted it and said "Typical… just when we had it in mind to get home, we're going to be killed by our own!"

The last plane seemed higher than the others, but when the bomb doors opened, a long, never-ending string of death poured from it. A few bombs fell short of the bridge. However, others dotted the mountainside until the bulk of them made a direct hit on the bridge. In less than a minute it had crashed into the valley floor like matchwood. The fast flowing river was taking it away as if it had never been there.

Once the raid was over, the Officers ordered prisoners to collect and bury their dead whilst the Thai natives were charged with helping any wounded guards. Alec and Ted were carrying stretchers and depositing the injured at the hospital.

On returning, they heard the Mackem from Sunderland shouting at them. "Hey fellas... help me up..."

They saw a bomb crater and there, not far from the edge under a mess of furniture from a broken-up hut, was Tommy. "That was a close one..."

His face was all black from the explosion and the boys began dragging stuff off him. "You'll have to speak up... I'm deaf! Tommy was lying face down, yet grinning like a fool.

"Just pull me out will you, I feel like I have half the mountain on my back!"

Suddenly Alec looked shocked. Ted registered his expression and walked back to where he was. Tommy's back had been broken by a table that had bent him in two. By far the worst was that the explosion had blown off both his legs and his vitals. The heat from the blast had cauterised the vast open wound. Without missing a beat, Alec seemed to know what to say.

"Hey, Tom we can't move some of that stuff... it's too heavy for us."

The last thing he wanted was for him to see that half of him was missing. Instead, they sat behind him and tried to keep his spirits up. They gave him bark to chew on and water to drink.

"Oh shit I'm dying aren't I?" said Tommy.

Their faces gave it away and they both began to weep.

Alec, as magnificent as ever, told a kindly lie. "No, but you need a bit of work my friend."

"Phew you had me worried there!" smiled Tommy. "I feel okay, my legs both hurt… are they trapped?"

A Japanese Officer approached, "Speedo."

He saw Tommy lying there and stared past the table to see that he had been blown apart. He walked around to Alec and Ted, pushing them away, telling them to get back to work. Both men backed off and shouted to Tommy that everything would be okay and they would be back.

Just then, the guard pushed a bayonet through Tommy's chest and stabbed again and again. Alec stared at him, his face contorted with tears and shock

"He didn't need to do that… he didn't need to that!"

Then, the only time in all those years, Alec lost it. "You bastard, you vicious, vicious bastard!"

Ignoring the man's rifle, he walked over to him and started punching him to ground. He wrestled the rifle from him and began battering him with the butt over and over again. Once he was certain he was dead, he threw the rifle away and marched into the centre parade ground shouting "Stop this… just stop this… we are fucking human beings!"

At that moment, he was hit on the back of the head with a club and dragged away. Ted stood there, two guards bayonets stopping him from following his friend.

The war was ending, everything he had wanted, but this was never part of the plan.

He felt alone, but not as lonely as Alec, roped to a hut and now confident he would never see his wife and children again.

Chapter 12

The camp had been put back together again.

Ted had not seen nor heard of Alec for weeks, presuming he had been shot. Everyone continued to be fed the same old rubbish rice and water.

Then one day, officers showed up and there, in front of Ted, was Alec being dragged by two bare-chested soldiers before being pushed onto his knees.

To Ted's surprise, he looked well.

Alec Smith, that gentle, kind and considerate Scot. The lives he had saved, the counsel he had given had made him a giant. His wife, Maggie and those two tiny children must surely be starting to forget what he had looked like. He was about six feet tall, sandy coloured hair and dark brown eyes.

Those eyes seemed to speak to him, all those things best friends never to say to one another, only feel. There were no closer friends on Earth, not after what they had gone through together.

There he was, on his knees with a soldier holding a long sword standing over him. The Officer's translator shouted,

"He killed a soldier of the magnificent Imperial Japanese Army, so must die."

The ranks, hardened to such things, stared on with eyes in starving boney sockets. Alec looked at Ted, nodded and said "Don't you dare... tell Maggie... you know!"

Tears rolled down Ted's cheeks as the sword fell and his best friend's head rolled down the yard, eventually stopping as if by choice so that he could keep in contact with his friend. There seemed to be a kind of link that lasted for minutes before Ted started to faint.

The translator told the prisoners that engineers would be arriving later that day to start rebuilding the bridge. This made everyone quiver in fear. Ted couldn't believe that circle of death was to begin again. His hut mates held him in place. Bill, the Aussie, dragged him back to the hut as the Japanese marched out of the camp.

———

As the sun reached its height in the sky, they noticed that there were no guards in camp. On the towers, the machine guns were unmanned. Just then a bugle was blown, playing assembly. This was the first time he had heard that since training in England.

The prisoners lined up in the parade area. An Aussie officer called Morrison said "It seems the Japanese have gone, rumours that the war is over may be true. However, we will gather whatever food we can get and have our first proper meal since we arrived here!"

A cheer went up, as Morrison urged caution "I've sent out a squad to find food and weapons for if the Japanese return, I suggest we fight"

Another huge cheer.

In some camps, the Japanese had remained behind until the Allied forces arrived. Here, everyone had left.

At the hospital, more men died, although the finding of a considerable supply of medical equipment and medicines probably saved a good dozen men who had been on the edge of oblivion.

Suddenly there was nothing but talk of home, places mentioned that few people had heard of; Wellington, Hybart, Alice Springs, while the Brit's mentioned Newcastle, Ipswich, Southport, Swansea and Dumfries. Just then, there was a furore from along the valley. For a split second, everyone thought the Japanese were returning. At the gate to the camp, three men had requisitioned Japanese rifles, ready to fight off the entire army if needs be.

They would never be prisoners again.

Then came the sound of bagpipes. A lad from Glasgow fell to his knees crying, "It's our boys.... shit.... its our boys!"

These human stick men, staggering on tiny starved legs, were cheering like a Cup Final crowd. In marched the parachute regiment, their medics careful not to give these sick and beaten men too much too soon for that would kill them.

That day they ate more than they had in years.

Paris had seen the worst of it across the Pacific, but on seeing the graves that stretched out as far as the eye could see, the newly arrived soldiers realised the gravity of these camps. There, trying to stand to attention to greet them, were a ragtag group of living skeletons, each one smiling and yet another third would never get home.

They were riddled with disease and would not be able to build up enough strength to win the fight to win back their lives.

The Americans were now flooding in with a few British

medics and a small detachment of British Troops. The Yanks spoke of the two bombs at Nagasaki and Hiroshima. Ted knew that those weapons had murdered millions of innocent men, women and children yet it had directly saved his life and the lives of many of his comrades in all the camps along the valley.

Bill had said "You Poms should come to Oz. It's hot and pretty this time of year."

Ted hugged him and they stayed like that for what seemed like an eternity.

The medics gave out salt tablets and water. Suddenly wagons started arriving to take people away.

Ted wrote:

"I remember thinking, this is my home. I had more memories from one single day in this camp than I had in my entire life before it. I was scared to leave, but climbed onto a truck and was gone, swept away singing 'It's a long way to Tipperary' with the boys"

As night approached, the sparkling stars seemed to guide their way as the sounds from the wild jungle full of creatures finally seemed to ebb. As they travelled, they would see the bodies of some of the Japanese who had fought right up until the end. Some of them had machine-gunned prisoners before seeking to flee. Two Japanese Officers had been hanged by prisoners near the gate to another Tamajao camp.

As the wagon bounced across the terrain, Ted wondered what would lie ahead.

Life could never be the same.

He would never see Bill again.

He never even found out if he made it back to Perth.

In November 1945, Ted Morris visited a street just out of Edinburgh centre to knock on the door of Maggie Smith. He was clutching in his hand dog tags, a tiny photograph and a million stories of heroism. The tears flowed and they hugged one another as Jean, now almost 6 and Alexander 9 learned about their Father…the hero.

Ted wrote:

"This was never really my story… it was Alec's."

THE END

Afterword

Eleven Days after the story was told, a postcard arrived from Kendal in Cumbria.

It read

"Thank you Alan, for what you did for my family. My Mam heard it four days before she died. It was as if she could not go until she did what she promised. Have given stuff to a museum. I will never be able to thank you enough!"

Signed Anth.

I have not heard from him since

I will forever be in his debt for him bringing such an incredible story to me and hope I did it justice.

Alan Robson MBE

About the Author

Alan Robson MBS is Britain's longest running Talk Show host. He has won more awards than any other broadcaster and is especially known for his interview technique and for hosting special shows involving the paranormal and esoteric. He qualified as an Exorcist in 2000 and is greatly loved by his audience of millions.

Despite offers from ALL the leading national players, Alan has remained as Metro Radio/TFM's flagship show for over 40 years, making it Britain's most listened to.

His first television show was 'PERSONAL CALL' with Nina Myskow. He then 17 series in a row on Tyne Tees/Yorkshire, including 'Robson's People' 7 series (12 episodes each), 'Robson's College Cuisine' (I series 18 episodes) and Trouble in Store BBC 1 (1 series 12 episodes).

American heavyweights, Fox became aware of his talents and hired him as host of 'SCARIEST PLACES ON EARTH' with Linda Blair. It became the most viewed 'phenomenon' show in the US and created so much interest Alan was invited onto 'LARRY KING LIVE' on CNN

In total, Alan hosted 3 massive series on Fox, then SYFY, Bravo and ABC.

His press career is equally impressive, with commissions for English speaking newspapers across the world, including being a regular in 'The Hong Kong Star' 'The Bangkok Press' and dozens of others worldwide.

The Sunday Sun hired him as 'Personal Columnist' for 11 years, following which he became a main feature writer for 13 years

The News Of The World regularly ran his ghost stories, including a month long series in their colour magazine of his 'GRISLY TALES'.

His book career has spanned decades following his original signing by Richard Branson. During this time, he wrote:-

GRISLY TRAILS & GHOSTLY TALES (No 1 Best Seller)

128,000 copies sold.

NIGHTMARE ON YOUR STREET (No1 Best Seller)

136,000 copies sold.

SIMPLY THE BEST (Christmas Joke Book) 76,000 copies sold.

THE LIVES AND LOVES OF A NIGHT OWL

(Hardback Autobiography) 56,000 copies sold.

For almost thirty years Alan hosted live gigs across the world, performing with Bob Dylan, Santana, Queen (5 times) ROD STEWART (3 times) BRYAN ADAMS (4 Times)

TINA TURNER (5 times) SIMPLY RED, DAVID BOWIE, GUN'S N ROSES and hundreds more.

He has appeared in countless pantomimes and was recently awarded the RADIO ACADEMY LIFETIME ACHIEVEMENT AWARD and given entry into NATIONAL RADIO HALL OF FAME

He was given an MBE from Her Majesty The Queen for services to broadcasting.

Alan lives in the North East of England.

www.robsonsworld.co.uk

Also by Alan Robson MBE

Walking in the Footsteps of Jack the Ripper

Grisly Trails and Ghostly Tales

Nightmare on Your Street; More Grisly Trails and Ghostly Tales

The Lives and Loves of a Night Owl (autobiography)

38133140R00044

Printed in Great Britain
by Amazon